Name CATH SHEPHERD

Address 51 MILLWOOD St

SHAWLANDS FLAT 1/2

G41 3JS

From

Date

# Book
*of*
# Prayers

**Carmelite Sisters**

*Carmelite Monastery*
*Glenvale*

# glenvale book of prayers

Inspired by the visit of the
Relics of St. Thérèse

© Copyright 2004
Carmelite Monastery Glenvale

Published by
Carmelite Monastery Glenvale
Newry Co.Down N.Ireland. BT34 2RD

We are grateful to Veritas for permission to include prayers
from the 'Alive O' programme

First published 2003
Reprinted 2004

ISBN No 0-9547434-0-7

Designed and produced by
B.J. McNally (Printers) 33 Patrick Street Newry BT35 8EB
(028) 3026 7413

Lord
Be my friend this day.
Help me to live as best I can.
Guide my steps along the way
And keep me always in your hand.

*St. Thérèse*

# List of Images

# contents

# praised be jesus christ

Dear Friends

We are pleased to present this book, which contains a choice of daily prayers and prayers for special intentions and occasions.

It was inspired by the visit of the Relics of St *Thérèse*. The photographs are from our chapel and grounds, which you can visit in person or in spirit. As a contemplative community we live a life of prayer and include special needs in our daily intercessions.

The prayers in this book could be helpful to parents who pray with their children, to couples who want to pray together and to those familiar with traditional prayers. Some people like to take a passage of scripture and reflect on it. Others pray in their own words. St Teresa tells us that 'prayer is intimate conversation with the one we know loves us'

May you find inspiration in the biblical and liturgical prayers in this book and consolation from our Lady or your favourite saint, in time of need. United with you in the kingdom of Jesus Christ on earth

*The Carmelite Sisters  Glenvale*

# SIGN OF THE CROSS

In the name of the Father
And of the Son
And of the Holy Spirit

Amen

The sign of the Cross is made at the beginning
and end of each period of prayer or at any time
when acknowledging the presence of God

# OUR FATHER

Our Father who art in Heaven
Hallowed be thy name
Thy Kingdom come
Thy will be done on earth
As it is in Heaven
Give us this day our daily bread
And forgive us our trespasses
As we forgive those who trespass against us
And lead us not into temptation
But deliver us from evil

Amen.

(Mt 6:9-14)

*Refer to page 95 for simple explanation of
the words of Our Father*

# HAIL MARY

Hail Mary full of grace
The Lord is with thee
Blessed art thou among women
and blessed is the fruit of thy womb, Jesus.
Holy Mary mother of God
Pray for us sinners,
Now and at the hour
of our death

Amen

*(Lk1:42)*

# GLORY BE TO THE FATHER

Glory be to the Father
and to the Son
and to the Holy Spirit.
As it was in the beginning
is now and ever shall be
world without end

Amen

# the apostles' creed

I believe in God, the Father almighty,
creator of heaven and earth.
I believe in Jesus Christ, his only Son, Our Lord,
He was conceived by the power
of the Holy Spirit
and born of the Virgin Mary.
He suffered under Pontius Pilate,
was crucified, died, and was buried.
He descended to the dead.
On the third day he rose again.
He ascended into heaven,
and is seated at the right hand of the Father.
He will come again to judge
the living and the dead.
I believe in the Holy Spirit,
the holy Catholic Church,
the communion of saints, the forgiveness of sins,
the resurrection of the body, and life everlasting.

Amen.

# CONFITEOR

I confess to almighty God,
and to you my brothers and sisters,
that I have sinned through my own fault
in my thoughts and in my words,
in what I have done,
and in what I have failed to do;
And I ask Blessed Mary, ever virgin,
All the angels and saints,
And you, my brothers and sisters,
To pray for me to the Lord our God.

Amen.

# MORNING PRAYER

Father in heaven, you love me,
You are with me night and day.
I want to love you always
In all I do and say.
I'll try to please you, Father,
Bless me through the day.

Amen.

# MORNING OFFERING

O Jesus, through the Immaculate Heart of Mary,
I offer you the prayers, works, joys and sufferings
of this day for all the intentions of your Sacred
Heart, in union with the holy sacrifice of the
Mass throughout the world.
And I offer them with the whole Church,
especially for the Pope's intentions.

Amen.

# A MORNING OFFERING

*(Composed by St. Thérèse)*

O My God! I offer you all my actions
of this day for the intentions and
for the glory of the Sacred Heart of Jesus.

I desire to sanctify every beat of my heart,
my every thought, my simplest works,
by uniting them to his infinite merits;
and I wish to make reparation for my sins
by casting them into that furnace
of his merciful love.

O my God! I ask of you for myself and those dear
to me the grace to fulfil perfectly your holy will,
to accept for love of you the joys and sorrows of
this passing life, so that we may one day be
united together in heaven for all eternity.

Amen.

# PRAYERS DURING
# the day

Lord Jesus,
I give you my hands to do your work.
I give you my feet to go your way.
I give you my eyes to see as you see.
I give you my tongue to speak your words.
I give you my mind that you might think in me.
I give you my spirit that you might pray in me.
Above all, I give you my heart,
that you may love in me, your
Father and all creation.
I give you my whole self, that you may grow in me,
so that it is you Lord Jesus,
who live and work and pray in me.

Direct Lord, we beseech you all our actions by your
holy inspirations and carry them on by your
gracious assistance, that every prayer and work of
ours may begin always from you
and by you be happily ended,
Through Christ our Lord
Amen.

# CONSECRATION TO OUR LADY

I choose you today, Mary, in the presence of the angels and the saints of heaven, for my Mother and my Queen. I consecrate to you, in obedience and love, all I am, and all the good I may do, putting myself and all that belongs to me entirely at your service, for the greater glory of God in time and in eternity.

*St Louis-Marie Grignion de Montfort*

Lord Jesus,
help me to spread your fragrance
everywhere I go;
Flood my soul with your Spirit and life;
Penetrate and possess my whole being so utterly
that all my life may only be a radiance of yours;
Shine through me and be so in me, that every
soul I come in contact with, may feel your
presence in my soul;
Let them look up and see no longer me,
but only Jesus.
Amen.

*Cardinal Newman*

# ST. PATRICKS BREASTPLATE

I bind onto myself today
The strong name of the Trinity
By invocation of the same
The Three in One and One in Three

Christ be with me, Christ be beside me,
Christ be before me, Christ be behind me,
Christ be at my right hand,
Christ be at my left hand,
Christ be with me everywhere I go,
Christ be my friend, for ever and ever.

Amen.

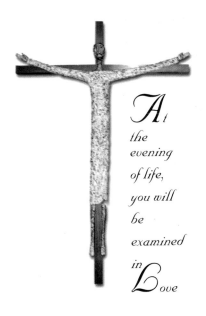

*At the evening of life, you will be examined in Love*

St. John of the Cross

# EVENING PRAYER

May he support us all the day long
till the shades lengthen and the evening comes
and the busy world is hushed and
the fever of life is over and our work is done;
then in his love and mercy may he give us a safe
lodging and a holy rest and peace at the last.

*(Cardinal Newman)*

Amen.

# ACT OF FAITH, HOPE AND CHARITY

O my God
I believe in you and in all you have revealed.
I hope in you and trust in your promises.
I love you above all things with all my
heart and soul and strength
and I love my neighbour as myself.

Amen.

# night prayer

God our Father, I come to say
Thank you for your love today.
Thank you for my family
And all the friends you give to me.
Guard me in the dark of night,
And in the morning send your light.
Amen.

# for protection

Blessed Michael the Archangel,
defend us in the hour of conflict.
Be our safeguard against the wickedness and
snares of the devil.
May God restrain him we humbly pray.
O Prince of the heavenly court
by the power of God thrust Satan down to hell
and with him all the other evil spirits who
wander through the world for the ruin of souls.

Amen.

# PRAYER TO
# ANGEL GUARDIAN

O Angel of God,
My Guardian dear,
to whom God's love
commits me here.
Ever this day (night)
be at my side,
to light and guard,
to rule and guide.

Amen.

# NIGHT BLESSINGS

Heart of Jesus, I adore you,
Heart of Mary, I implore you.
Heart of Joseph, pure and just,
in these three hearts,
I put my trust.  Amen.


Save us Lord while we are awake,
protect us while we sleep,
that we may keep watch with Christ
and rest with him in peace.  Amen


Into your hands O great God,
I commend my spirit.
Lord Jesus receive my soul.


May the Lord grant us a quiet night
and a perfect end.  Amen.

# GRACE
# BEFORE MEALS

Bless us, O God, as we sit together.
Bless the food we eat today.
Bless the hands that made the food.
Bless us, O God.

Amen.

# GRACE
# AFTER MEALS

Thank you, God, for the food we have eaten.
Thank you, God for all our friends.
Thank you, God for everything.
Thank you, God.

Amen.

# traditional
# GRACE BEFORE meals

Bless us O Lord and these your gifts
which of your bounty
we are about to receive
Through Christ our Lord

Amen.

# traditional
# GRACE after meals

We give you thanks Almighty God
for all your blessings
which we have received
Through Christ our Lord

Amen.

# PRAYER BEFORE THE SACRAMENT OF PENANCE

God our Father, help me to
remember the times when
I didn't live as Jesus asked me to.
Help me to be sorry and to try again.
Amen.

# PRAYER AFTER THE SACRAMENT OF PENANCE

God our Father, thank you for forgiving me.
Help me to love others.
Help me to live as Jesus asked me to.
Amen.

# act of sorrow

O my God, I thank you for loving me.
I am sorry for all my sins;
For not loving others and not loving you.
Help me to live like Jesus and not sin again.
Amen.

# act of contrition

O my God,
I am very sorry
for having sinned against you.
Because you are so good and
with the help of your grace,
I will not sin again.
Amen.

# SCRIPTURE READING FOR EXAMINATION OF CONSCIENCE

*Be ambitious for the higher gifts. And I am going to show you a way that is better than any of them. Love is always patient and kind; it is never jealous. Love is never boastful or conceited; it is never rude or selfish; it does not take offence and is not resentful. Love takes no pleasure in other people's sins but delights in the truth; it is always ready to excuse, to trust, to hope and to endure whatever comes.*

*Love does not come to an end. But if there are gifts of prophecy, the time will come when they must fail; or the gift of languages, it will not continue for ever; and knowledge - for this, too, the time will come when it must fail. For our knowledge is imperfect and our prophesying is imperfect; but once perfection comes, all imperfect things will disappear.*

*In short, there are three things that last; faith, hope and love; and the greatest of these is love.*

(1 Cor 12:31;13:4-13)

# examination of conscience

**(based on 1 Cor :13)**

When we come to examine our conscience we can:

- First of all thank God for what he has done for us.

- Consider what God might thank us for.

- Think of the things we could have done better.

1. *What are the things we can thank God for?*
   The obvious ones.... life, health, home, family, friends, job, neighbours, talents, school.

2. *What are the things God might thank us for?*
   For doing our best with the talents we have, for doing our best at home, at school or at work, or for being honest and hardworking, just and generous.

3. *What are the things we could have done better?*
   We know that there are different gifts but always the same Spirit.

- Do I use my talents well or do I use them selfishly, just to further my own career or gain more money or possessions?

- Do I share what I have with my family and those who are less well off?

- Am I selfish with my time and talents?

- *Love is patient and kind* - Am I patient and kind within my own home and workplace?

- *Love is never jealous* - Am I jealous of others gifts and talents and possessions?

- *Love is not boastful or conceited* - Do I like to boast and exaggerate my importance?

- *Love is never rude or selfish.* Am I rude to others, do I bully or try to get my own way? Do I gossip and discredit others? Am I selfish?

- *Love does not take offence or store up grievances*
  Do I huff and seek revenge? Do I have an
  'I will get my own back' attitude?

- *Love does not rejoice at wrongdoing but finds its
  joy in the truth*
  Am I truthful? Do I pray for others? Do I
  pray at all?

- *Love is always ready to make allowances, to
  trust, to hope and to endure whatever comes*
  Do I get angry and revengeful when things do
  not go my way? Am I trustworthy?

- *These remain, faith, hope and love and the
  greatest of these is love*
  How do I love? Is my love genuine, pure,
  moral, selfgiving, supportive?

# the greatest commandment

*Master, which is the greatest commandment of the Law?' Jesus said, 'you must love the Lord your God with all your heart, with all your soul and with all your mind. This is the greatest and first commandment. The second resembles it: you must love your neighbour as yourself.*

(Mt 22:35-39)

# examination of conscience based on
# the ten commandments

1. I am the Lord your God,
   you shall not have strange gods before me.

2. You shall not take the name of the Lord your
   God in vain.

3. Remember to keep holy the Lord's Day.

4. Honour your father and mother.

5. You shall not kill.

6. You shall not commit adultery.

7. You shall not steal.

8. You shall not bear false witness against your
   neighbour.

9. You shall not covet your neighbour's wife.

10. You shall not covet your neighbour's goods.

*(Exodus 20:1-17)*

# the eight beatitudes

1. Blessed are the pure in spirit, for theirs is the kingdom of heaven.

2. Blessed are those who mourn, for they shall be comforted.

3. Blessed are the meek, for they shall inherit the earth.

4. Blessed are those who hunger and thirst for righteousness for they shall be satisfied.

5. Blessed are the merciful, for they shall obtain mercy.

6. Blessed are the pure in heart for they shall see God.

7. Blessed are the peacemakers for they shall be called children of God.

8. Blessed are those who are persecuted for righteousness' sake for theirs is the kingdom of heaven.

*(Mt. 5:1-12)*

# penitential psalm

*O GOD HAVE MERCY ON ME*     PSALM 50

Have mercy on me, God, in your kindness.
In your compassion blot out my offence.
O wash me more and more from my guilt
and cleanse me from my sin.

My offences truly I know them;
my sin is always before me.
Against you, you alone, have I sinned;
what is evil in your sight I have done.

That you may be justified when you give sentence
and be without reproach when you judge.
O see, in guilt I was born,
a sinner was I conceived.

Indeed you love truth in the heart;
then in the secret of my heart teach me wisdom.
O purify me, then I shall be clean;
O wash me, I shall be whiter than snow.

Make me hear rejoicing and gladness,
that the bones you have crushed may revive.
From my sins turn away your face
and blot out all my guilt.

A pure heart create for me, O God,
put a steadfast spirit within me.
Do not cast me away from your presence,
nor deprive me of your Holy Spirit.

Give me again the joy of your help;
with a spirit of fervour sustain me,
that I may teach transgressors your ways
and sinners may return to you.

O rescue me, God my helper,
and my tongue shall ring out your goodness.
O Lord, open my lips
and my mouth shall declare your praise.

# stations of the cross

1.  JESUS IS CONDEMNED TO DEATH
    *(Prayer at each station)*
    We adore you O Christ and we bless you,
    Because by your holy cross you have
    redeemed the world.
    or
    Lord, by your cross and resurrection you
    have set us free. You are the Saviour of the
    world.
    *(Our Father and a Hail Mary)*

2.  JESUS RECEIVES THE CROSS

3. JESUS FALLS THE FIRST TIME

4. JESUS MEETS HIS MOTHER

5. SIMON HELPS TO CARRY THE CROSS OF JESUS

6. VERONICA WIPES THE FACE OF JESUS

7. JESUS FALLS THE SECOND TIME

8. JESUS MEETS THE WOMEN OF JERUSALEM

9. JESUS FALLS THE THIRD TIME

10. JESUS IS STRIPPED OF HIS GARMENTS

11. JESUS IS NAILED TO THE CROSS

12. JESUS DIES ON THE CROSS

13. JESUS IS TAKEN DOWN FROM THE CROSS

14. JESUS IS LAID IN THE TOMB

JESUS IS RAISED FROM THE DEAD

# PRAYERS BEFORE COMMUNION

Lord Jesus, come to me.
Lord Jesus, give me your love,
Lord Jesus, come to me and give me yourself.

Lord Jesus, friend of children, come to me.
Lord Jesus, you are my Lord and my God.
Praise to you, Lord Jesus Christ.

Amen.

# PRAYERS AFTER COMMUNION

Lord Jesus I love and adore you,
You are a special friend to me.
Welcome, Lord Jesus, O welcome.
Thank you for coming to me.

Thank you, Lord Jesus, O thank you,
For giving yourself to me.
Make me strong to show your love,
Wherever I may be.

I'm ready now, Lord Jesus,
To show how much I care.
I'm ready now to give your love
at home and everywhere.

Be near me, Lord Jesus, I ask you to stay.
Close by me forever, and love me, I pray.
Bless all of us children in your loving care,
And bring us to heaven to live with you there.

Amen.

# COMMUNION REFLECTION

## FROM THE WRITINGS OF ST. TERESA OF AVILA

When you have received the Lord and are in his presence, try to shut the bodily eyes and open the eyes of the soul.

Do not lose such an excellent time for talking with Our Lord as the hour after Holy Communion. This is a good time for our Master to teach us and for us to listen to him. Beg him to show you how to pray and never to leave you.

We have no need to go and seek him somewhere a long way off. Delight to remain with him. Pray to him. Talk to him. It is as if we saw the Lord entering our poor abode. Let us enter into that abode with him.

If while Our Lord went about in the world, the sick were healed merely by touching his clothes how can we doubt that he will work miracles when he is within us? He will give us what we ask of him since he is in our house.

Oh my Lord, how little we profit from the
blessings which you have granted us. Your
majesty seeks methods and ways and inventions
by which to show us what love you have for us.
Blessed forever so great a God.

Amen.

# ANIMA CHRISTI

Soul of Christ, sanctify me.
Body of Christ, save me.
Blood of Christ, inebriate me.
Water from the side of Christ, wash me.
Passion of Christ, strengthen me.
O good Jesus, hear me.
Hide me within your wounds.
Never let me be separated from you.
From the malignant enemy defend me.
At the hour of my death call me,
And bid me come to you,
So that with your saints I may praise you for ever.
Amen

*As they were eating Jesus took some bread, and
when he said the blessing he broke it and gave it to
his disciples, "Take it and eat it" he said, " this is my
body". Then he took the cup and when he had
received thanks he gave it to them, " drink all of you
from this" he said, "this is my blood, the blood of the
covenant, which is to be poured out for many for the
forgiveness of sins.*

(Mt:26: 26-28)

# EN EGO
## [PRAYER BEFORE A CRUCIFIX]

Behold, O kind and most sweet Jesus, I cast myself on my knees in your sight, and with the most fervent desire of my soul, I pray and beseech you that you would impress upon my heart lively sentiments of faith, hope and charity, with a true repentance of my sins, and a firm desire of amendment, while with deep affection and grief of soul I ponder within myself and mentally contemplate your five most precious wounds; having before my eyes that which David spoke in prophecy of you, O good Jesus:
*'They pierced my hands and my feet; they have numbered all my bones'.*

# COMHARTHA NA CROISE

In ainm an Athar,
Agus an Mhic
Agus an Spioraid Naoimh.

Amen.

# GLÓIR DON ATHAIR

Glóir don Athair,
Agus don Mhac,
Agus don Spioraid Naomh.
Mar a bhí ó thús,
Mar atá anois,
Agus mar a bheas go brách
Le saol na saol.

Amen.

# ár nathair

Ár nAthair, atá ar neamh,
Go naofar d'ainm,
Go dtaga do ríocht,
Go ndéantar do thoil ar an talamh,
Mar a dhéantar ar neamh.
Ár n-arán laethúil tabhair dúinn inniu,
Agus maith dúinn ár bhfiacha,
Mar a mhaithimidne dár bhféichiúna féin,
Agus ná lig sinn i gcathú,
Ach saor sinn ó olc.

Amen.

# SÉ DO BHEATHA, A MHUIRE

Sé do bheatha, a Mhuire,
Atá lán de ghrásta,
Tá an Tiarna leat.
Is beannaithe thú idir mhná,
agus is beannaithe toradh do bhroinne, Íosa.
A Naomh-Mhuire, a Mhathair Dé,
Guí orainn, na peacaigh,
anois agus ar uair ár mbáis.

Amen.

# THE ROSARY

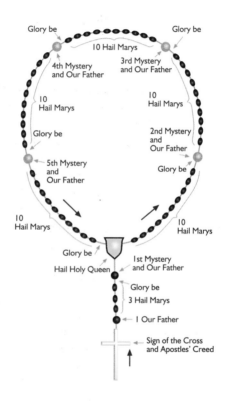

# the ROSARY

(Extract from the Apostolic Letter of Pope John Paul II *'Rosarium Virginis Mariae'* on the Rosary 2002)

To recite the Rosary is to contemplate with Mary the life, death and resurrection of Jesus, her Son. The Rosary is Mary's memories. The memories of Jesus impressed upon her heart were always with her, leading her to reflect on the various moments of her life at her Son's side. By its nature the recitation of the Rosary calls for a quiet rhythm and a lingering pace, helping the individual to meditate on the mysteries of the Lord's life as seen through the eyes of Mary.

No one knows Christ better than Mary; no one can introduce us to a profound knowledge of his mystery better than his mother. If Jesus is the Way, Mary shows us the Way. The Rosary is both meditation and supplication. It is a prayerful presentation of the mysteries of Christ.

# the
# JOYFUL MYSTERIES

*Monday and Saturday*

The first five decades, the joyful mysteries are marked by the joy, mixed with drama, radiating from the event of Jesus' Incarnation.

1. **THE ANNUNCIATION** *(Lk 1:26-38)*
2. **THE VISITATION** *(Lk 1:39-56)*
3. **THE NATIVITY** *(Lk 2:1-20)*
4. **THE PRESENTATION** *(Lk 2:22-38)*
5. **FINDING IN THE TEMPLE** *(Lk 2:41-52)*

Easter Sunday

YEAR 2

...ing to Mark

GOSPEL

(16:1-8)

amazed. And he said to them, 'Do not be amazed; you seek Jesus of Nazareth, who was crucified. He has risen, he is not here; see the place where they laid him. But go, tell his disciples...

# the
# mysteries of light

*(New mysteries introduced by Pope John Paul II)*
*Thursday*

Moving from the infancy and hidden life of Nazareth to the public life of Jesus our contemplation brings us to those mysteries which may be called in a special way 'mysteries of light'

1. **THE BAPTISM OF JESUS** *(Mt 3:13-17)*

2. **THE WEDDING FEAST OF CANA** *(Jn 2:1-12)*

3. **THE PROCLAMATION OF THE KINGDOM AND CALL TO CONVERSION** *(Mk 1:14-15; 2:3-13)*

4. **THE TRANSFIGURATION** *(Lk 9:28-36)*

5. **THE INSTITUTION OF THE EUCHARIST** *(Mt 26:26-29)*

# the
# SORROWFUL MYSTERIES

*Tuesday and Friday*

The Rosary selects certain moments from the
Passion, inviting us to contemplate them in our
hearts. The sorrowful mysteries help us to relive
the death of Jesus, to stand at the foot of the
cross beside Mary, to enter into the depths of
God's love for us and to experience all its life
giving power.

1. THE AGONY IN THE GARDEN *(Lk 22:39-44)*
2. THE SCOURGING AT THE PILLAR  *(Lk 23:1-22)*
3. THE CROWNING WITH THORNS *(Mk 15:15-20)*
4. THE CARRYING OF THE CROSS *(Lk 23:26-34)*
5. THE CRUCIFIXION *(Lk 23:34-46)*

# the GLORIOUS MYSTERIES

*Wednesday and Sunday*

Jesus is the Risen One. The rosary invites us to pass beyond the darkness of the Passion in order to gaze upon Christ's glory. Mary was there at the coming of the Holy Spirit and she herself is given the unique privilege of the assumption into Heaven and being crowned in glory. She shines forth as Queen of Angels and Saints, Heaven and Earth, in anticipation of the glory that awaits all of us as followers of Christ and members of the Church.

1. **THE RESURRECTION** (Mk 16:1-8)

2. **THE ASCENSION** (Acts 1:6-11)

3. **THE DESCENT OF THE HOLY SPIRIT** (Acts 2:1-12)

4. **THE ASSUMPTION OF MARY INTO HEAVEN** (1 Th 4:13-18)

5. **THE CROWNING OF MARY QUEEN OF HEAVEN** (Rev 12:1; 14:1-5)

# the our father

In each of his mysteries, Jesus leads us to the Father. By virtue of his relationship to the Father he makes us brothers and sisters of himself and of one another.

# the 10 hail marys

The first part of the Hail Mary is drawn from the words spoken to Mary by the Angel Gabriel (at the Annunciation) and by St Elizabeth (at the Visitation). The centre of gravity in the Hail Mary, the hinge as it were which joins its two parts, is the name of JESUS. From Mary's unique privileged relationship with Christ, which makes her the Mother of God, derives the forcefulness of the appeal we make to her in the second half of the prayer, as we entrust to her maternal intercession our lives and the hour of our death.

# GLORY BE TO THE FATHER

Christ is the way that leads us to the Father in
the Spirit. Trinitarian doxology is the goal of all
Christian contemplation. In public recitation of
the Rosary it is recommended that the Glory be
to the Father should be sung.

# THE ROSARY BEADS

The traditional aid used for the recitation of the
Rosary is the set of beads. The beads converge
upon the Crucifix. The life and prayer of
believers is centred upon Christ. The beads are a
'chain' which links us with Mary and with Christ.

The Rosary is by its nature a prayer for peace. As
a prayer for peace it is also and always has been a
prayer of and for the family. It is also beautiful
and fruitful to entrust to this prayer the growth
and development of children. To pray the Rosary
for children and even more with children is a
spiritual aid which should not be underestimated.

*'Rosarium Virginis Mariae'*      *Pope John Paul II*

49

# the hail holy queen

Hail Holy Queen,
Mother of Mercy
Hail our life our sweetness and our hope.
To you do we cry,
poor banished children of Eve,
To you do we send up our sighs,
Mourning and weeping in this valley of tears
Turn then most gracious advocate
your eyes of mercy towards us
And after this our exile show onto us
the blessed fruit of your womb, Jesus
Oh clement, Oh loving, Oh sweet Virgin Mary
Pray for us, Oh Holy Mother of God
That we may be made worthy
of the promises of Christ.

# PRAYER AFTER ROSARY

O God, whose only-begotten Son, by his life,
death and resurrection, has purchased for us the
rewards of eternal life; grant, we beseech you,
that meditating upon these mysteries of the
Most Holy Rosary of the Blessed Virgin Mary, we
may imitate what they contain,
and obtain what they promise
through the same Christ our Lord.

Amen

May the divine assistance remain always with us.
And may the souls of the faithful departed,
through the mercy of God, rest in peace.

Amen

# the angelus

V. The angel of the Lord declared unto Mary,
R. And she conceived of the Holy Spirit.
Hail Mary.....

V. Behold the handmaid of the Lord,
R. Be it done unto me according to your word.
Hail Mary....

V. And the Word was made flesh
R. And dwelt among us.
Hail Mary....

V. Pray for us, O Holy Mother of God,
R. That we may be made worthy of the promises
of Christ.

*(Said at 6.00 a.m., 12 noon and 6.00 p.m.
when the Angelus bell is rung)*

Let us Pray
Pour forth we beseech O Lord,
your grace into our hearts,
that we to whom the incarnation
of Christ your Son was made known
by the message of an angel,
may by his passion and cross
be brought to glory of his resurrection.
Through the same Christ our Lord

Amen.

# novena prayers
# and
# prayers for
# special occasions

# the memorare

Remember O most gracious Virgin Mary,
that never was it known, that anyone who fled
to your protection, implored your help,
or sought your intercession, was left unaided.
Inspired with this confidence I fly unto you,
O Virgin of Virgins my Mother;
to you I come; before you I stand;
sinful and sorrowful
O Mother of the Word Incarnate despise
not my petitions, but in your mercy
hear and answer me.
Amen

# christmas novena

Hail and blessed be the hour and moment in
which the Son of God was born of the most pure
Virgin Mary at midnight in Bethlehem in
piercing cold. In that hour, vouchsafe, O my God
to hear my prayer and grant my desires, through
the merits of our Saviour Jesus Christ and of his
Blessed Mother (Make petition)
Amen

# the sacred heart

You have said, O Divine Jesus,
*Ask and you will receive, seek and you will find, knock
and it will be opened to you.*
Relying on these promises,
I come with confidence to beg of you
the favours that I need.

*(Requests)*
From whom shall I ask, Lord Jesus,
if not from you, whose heart is an unfailing source
of graces and merits?
Most loving Heart of my God,
I believe in your power;
I believe in your knowledge,
I believe in your personal love for me.
Therefore O Sacred Heart of Jesus,
I place all my trust in you.

Amen.

# OUR LADY OF MOUNT CARMEL

O most beautiful flower
of Carmel, Fruitful Vine,
Splendour of Heaven,
Blessed Mother of the
Son of God, Immaculate Virgin,
assist me in this my time of need.
O Star of the Sea help me and show me that you
are my Mother.

O Holy Mary Mother of God,
Queen of Heaven and Earth,
I humbly beseech you from the bottom of my
heart to assist me in this my hour of need.
O show me that you are my Mother.

O Mary conceived without sin,
pray for us who have recourse to you.

Amen.

# SAINT JOSEPH

Remember, O glorious St Joseph,
that never was it know that anyone
had recourse to your protection,
implored your help, or sought your intercession
without obtaining relief.
Confiding, therefore, in your goodness,
I come into your presence
and fervently recommend myself
to your care and protection.
Despise not, most loving father
of my Redeemer, my petition....
but graciously hear and grant it.

Amen.

*St. Joseph, pray for us.*

# the child of prague

O Child Jesus, I have recourse to you;
I implore you to assist me in this necessity...
I confidently hope to obtain your holy grace.
I love you with my whole heart
and my whole soul.
I am heartily sorry for my sins,
and I entreat you, O good Jesus,
to give me strength to overcome them.
Henceforward I wish to serve you faithfully.
For the love of you, O Divine Child,
I will love my neighbour as myself.
O Jesus, most powerful Child,
I again implore you
to assist me on this occasion...
Grant me the grace of possessing you
eternally with Mary and Joseph.

Amen.

*Divine Child Jesus, assist us.*

# st. thérèse of lisieux

O Little Thérèse of the Child Jesus, who during your short life on earth became a mirror of angelic purity, of love strong as death and of wholehearted abandonment to God, now that you rejoice in the reward of your virtues, cast a glance of pity on me and listen to my prayer. I leave everything in your hands. Make my troubles your own. Speak a word for me to Our Lady Immaculate - to the Queen of Heaven who smiled on you at dawn of life. Beg her as Queen of the Heart of Jesus, to obtain for me by her powerful intercession the grace I yearn for so ardently at this moment. *(Petition)* And beg her to join with it a blessing that may strengthen me during life, defend me at the hour of death, and lead me to a happy eternity.

Amen.

*Little Flower show your power
every hour for Jesus' sake*

# PRAYER OF ST. THÉRÈSE

Lord, give me the open heart of a child. Let me come trustingly to you, not afraid to ask for your love. Deliver me from the belief that I am self-sufficient. Show me my need of you. Give me the grace to reach out to you. Lord, give me a child's simplicity and a sense  of wonder. May my enthusiasm for you never dim. Let me hasten to converse with you in the intimacy of prayer. Give me discernment to realise there is no detail of my life too tiny for your concern. Help me to perceive your glory in the helplessness of the cross. Son of God, who for my sake, took on the dependency of childhood, help me to accept the readiness of the Father's grace.

Amen.

# PRAYER OF ST. FRANCIS

LORD, make me an instrument of your peace
Where there is hatred, let me sow love;
where there is injury, pardon;
where there is doubt, faith;
where there is despair, hope;
where there is darkness, light;
and where there is sadness, joy.

O DIVINE MASTER, grant that I may not
so much seek to be consoled as to console;
to be understood as to understand;
to be loved as to love;
for it is in giving that we receive,
it is in pardoning that we are pardoned,
and it is in dying that we are
born to eternal life.

# PRAYER TO OUR LADY OF LOURDES

O ever Immaculate Virgin, Mother of mercy,
health of the sick, refuge of sinners,
comfort of the afflicted - you know our wants,
our troubles, our sufferings.
Look on us with love and pity.
You appeared at the Grotto of Lourdes
and made it a holy sanctuary
of prayer and healing grace.

Many sufferers have already
been healed in soul and body.
We come, therefore, with complete confidence
to implore your intercession.
O most loving Mother, obtain for us
the graces we ask for..........
We will endeavour always to imitate
your virtues that we may one day
rejoice with you in the glory of heaven.

Amen.

O Mary conceived without sin, pray for us who
have recourse to you.
Blessed be the holy and Immaculate Conception
of the Most Blessed Virgin Mary.

*St. Bernadette, Pray for us*

# ST. TERESA OF AVILA'S BOOKMARK

Let nothing disturb you
Let nothing frighten you
All things pass away
God never changes
Patience obtains all things
Those who have God
find they lack nothing.
God alone suffices.

Amen.

# st. anthony
## of
## padua

(To find lost objects)

O good St. Anthony, who has
received from God a special power
to find lost things, help me find
what I am seeking for and to give
thanks when it is recovered.

May Mary and Joseph, who
searched for Jesus for three days
help me now in my search.

Amen

# the holy trinity

O Blessed Trinity, I adore you.
Help me to forget myself that I may be rooted
in you as still and as peaceful as if my soul were
already in eternity. May nothing disturb my
peace or make me leave you. May I enter into
the depths of your mystery. Give peace to my
soul and make it your heaven, your dwelling and
your resting place. May I never leave you there
alone but may I be present in faith and adoration
and surrendered to your creative action. O my
Three, my Trinity, my All, my infinite solitude, I
surrender myself to you, until I depart to
contemplate you in eternity.

Amen

*(Blessed Elizabeth of the Trinity's prayer adapted)*

# DIVINE MERCY

### The Chaplet of Divine Mercy
*(The chaplet can be said on ordinary Rosary Beads)*

Our Father, Hail Mary and the Creed

**On large beads:**
Eternal Father, I offer you the Body and Blood,
Soul and Divinity of your dearly beloved Son,
Our Lord Jesus Christ, in atonement for our sins
and those of the whole world.

**On the small beads:**
For the sake of his sorrowful Passion have mercy
on us and the whole world.

**Conclude with:**
Holy God, Holy Mighty One, Holy Immortal
One, have mercy on us and on the whole world.
(three times)

# PRAYER TO THE HOLY SPIRIT

Come, Holy Spirit, fill the hearts of
your faithful
And kindle in them the fire of your love.

Send forth your Spirit, and they shall
be created
And you will renew the face of the earth.

Let us Pray:

O God who by the light of the Holy Spirit
instructs the hearts of the faithful.
Grant that by the gift of the same Divine Spirit
we may have a right understanding in all things
and ever rejoice in his holy consolations
through Christ our Lord.

Amen.

# PRAYER FOR GUIDANCE

Father, I am seeking,
I am hesitant and uncertain,
but will you, O God,
watch over each step of mine
and guide me.

*St Augustine*

Lord
Let me do your will;
make your way plain for me to follow.

*Psalm 5*

# FOR EXAMS

Our Lady
our Queen and our Mother
in the name of Jesus
and for the love of Jesus
we implore you to take
our cause in your hands
and grant us good success.

# PRAYER OF AN EXPECTANT MOTHER

God our Father, as you are giving me the
blessing of bringing an infant into the
world and knowing that as Creator of all life
it is more truly yours than mine, I ask you to
help me to fulfil all my maternal duties.

O Lord Jesus Christ, look upon this unborn
little one that lies close to my heart. Grant
that this baby may one day become a member
of the Church through the sacrament of Baptism.

Holy Spirit, sanctify us, father, mother and baby.
Holy Mary, Mother of God nourish us with your
love and protection always.

Dear St. Joseph, watch over our baby as you
watched over Jesus.
Holy angel of our little child, pray for us.

Amen.

# BLESSING OF BABY

*Jesus said;*
*Let the children come to me, for it is to*
*such as these that the kingdom of God belongs.*
*Then he put his arms round them, laid his hands on*
*them and gave them his blessing* (Mk 10:13-16)

Make the sign of the Cross on your child's
forehead and pray, expressing your hopes and
dreams, desires and wishes for him/her.

# FAMILY PRAYER

*When they had done everything the Law of*
*the Lord required Joseph and Mary went back*
*to Galilee to their own town of Nazareth.*
*Meanwhile the child, Jesus, grew to maturity*
*and he was filled with wisdom and God's favour was*
*with him.* (Lk 2:39,40)

May God's favour rest on our child/children
May they grow in wisdom and grace,
May they be safe from all evil and harm and
May they be guided by the Holy Spirit
in all their life's decisions. Amen

# PRAYER FOR PARENTS

God our Father, I thank you for having given us
Louis and Zelie Martin.  United and faithful in
marriage, they have left us an example of
Christian living and evangelical virtue.  In raising
a large family through trials, suffering and
bereavement, they put their trust in you and
always sought your will.

Make known your will in their regard and grant
the favour I ask..........in the hope that the father
and mother of St. Thérèse of the Child Jesus may
one day be held up by the Church as a model for
the families of our time.

Amen.

# FOR SINGLE PEOPLE

Lord, in the spirit of the Beatitudes we are called
to live our vocation in the church.
Fill us with courage in loneliness and peace in
our work that we may reflect your life in ours
and enrich this world
with the talents you have given us.

# FOR LOVED ONES FAR AWAY

Guard O Sacred Heart of Jesus
All our loved ones far away
Shield them in their hour of need
And keep them in your ways.
Amen

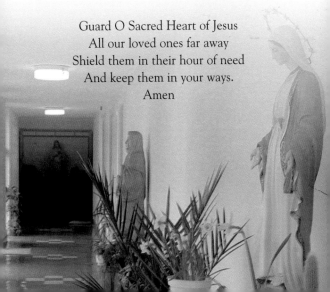

# PRAYER FOR WORKERS
## and for those seeking employment

God our Creator, by our labour you govern
and bring to perfection the work of creation.
Hear our prayers, give all people work that
enhances human dignity and draw us closer
to each other in service and justice.

*Jesus said:*
*Come to me all you who labour and are overburdened*
*and I will give you rest.*
*Shoulder my yoke and learn from me for*
*I am gentle and humble of heart and*
*you will find rest for your souls. Yes my*
*yoke is easy and my burden light.*

(Mt 11: 28-30)

# PRAYER FOR LEISURE TIME

God our Father in your work of creation
you have given us a time for everything
and therefore we thank you for our leisure
time. May our music and our games, our
art and entertainment give you glory and
praise and lead us to acknowledge you as
the source of all good and beauty. We ask
this through Christ our Lord. Amen.

*When I see the heavens, the work of your hands*
*The moon and the stars which you arranged*
*What are we that you should keep us in mind*
*mortal people that you care for us.*
*Yet you have made us little less than a god*
*with glory and honour you crowned us, gave us power*
*over the works of your hand put all things under our*
*feet*
*How great is your name O Lord our God*
*through all the earth*

*(Psalm 8)*

# for teachers

*Joseph and Mary found Jesus in the temple among the teachers, listening to them and asking them questions. (Lk: 2:46)*

Come Holy Spirit, guide and enlighten all teachers that they may impart God's wisdom and understanding to our young people. May they help them in their quest for knowledge and in living just and upright lives. Spirit of wisdom and understanding fall afresh on them.

# for parish renewal

God our Father, you have given us the gift of life and called us to follow your Son, Jesus. May we learn from him how to love you and all that you have created. May we know the power of the Holy Spirit in our hearts, in our homes and in our communities. Teach us to be open to your word and attentive to the needs of our brothers and sisters. Guide our search for ways in which we can show your compassionate love in our world. Through the intercession of Mary and of our patron Saint N we make this prayer through Christ our Lord. Amen

# FOR PRIESTS AND RELIGIOUS

God our Father we give you thanks for the priests and religious who serve you in the Church. Bless and confirm them in their calling. Give them the faith, hope and love they need to be your witnesses to the truth of the Gospel message.

# FOR MISSIONARIES

Father, you make your name known throughout the world, through the Christian zeal and apostolic work of missionaries. By the help of our prayers may they be strengthened and encouraged to spread the Good News of Jesus Christ.

# FOR VOCATIONS

God our Father, send workers into your harvest. Give them the gifts they need to respond generously and with joyful hears to the service of Christ and his Church.

*When he saw the crowds, Jesus felt sorry for them because they were harassed and dejected, like sheep without a shepherd. Then he said to his disciples; the harvest is rich but the labourers are few. So ask the Lord of the harvest to send labourers to his harvest.* (Mt 9:36-37)

# SERENITY PRAYER

God
grant me the serenity
to accept the things I cannot change,
courage to change the thing I can,
and the wisdom to know the difference.

# PRAYER OF ABANDONMENT

Father, I abandon myself into you hands;
Do with me what you will.
Whatever you may do, I thank you;
I am ready for all, I accept all.
Let only your will be done in me and in all your
creatures.
Into your hands I commend my soul:
I offer it to you with all the love of my heart, for
I love you, Lord, and so need to give myself,
to surrender myself into your hands without
reserve and with boundless confidence, for you
are my Father.

*Charles de Foucauld*

# FOR DOCTORS AND NURSES

*Jesus said;*
*This is my commandment; love one another as I*
*have loved you.* (Jn: 15:12)

Lord give doctors and nurses love in their hearts
and skill in their hands to heal and comfort all
those bruised and broken by illness or old age.
Mary, comforter of the afflicted, pray for them.

# FOR THE ABUSED AND THOSE WHO SUFFER INJUSTICE

*Jesus said; Love your enemies, do good to those who*
*hate you, bless those who curse you, pray for those*
*who treat you badly. Treat others as you would like*
*them to treat you.* (Lk 6:27,31)

Lord it is difficult to forgive and to live with
shame and pain. It is hard to take up the broken
pieces and the shattered trusts and to go on to
hope that life can be freed from darkness and
despair. May the light of your love melt the
stone of fear in our hearts. Jesus, who suffered
scourging and mockery, save us from injustice
and give us peace and hope.

Amen.

# A PRAYER FOR HEALING

Lord, I come now before you in the weakness
that has overcome me, with the feelings that I
cannot share and try to hide, with the emptiness
that sometimes grips me, and with the physical
and mental pain that so often preoccupies me,
but I also come in faith and trust, in humility and
reverence, and I ask to be relieved and healed.

You took human weakness on yourself when you
lived, suffered and died for our sake. By rising
from the dead, you manifested your victory over
all human weakness, over all the negatives that
tend to break us, and over death itself. Because
of that our trust in you is deepened. You can
overcome the negative feelings we experience.

Now I present myself to you, knowing that you
love me just as I am, but knowing also that your
will is my happiness and that you can bring this
about in ways that I will not be able to
understand.

Help me this day not to be undermined by illness, by pain, or by the problems that beset me. I ask this, not just for myself but for the sake of all those whose lives I touch.

Amen.

*Brian McNamara SJ*

# IN TIME OF SORROW

*(Prayer of St. Edith Stein)*
Today I have stood with you beneath the Cross
And felt more certainly than ever before,
That you became our Mother beneath the Cross.
How faithfully an earthly mother strives
To fulfil her dying son's last wish.

But you were the handmaid of the Lord.
Subduing wholly your own life and being
To the life and being of God incarnate.
You have taken your own to your heart
And with your heart bleeding from bitter sorrow
Have purchased for each one of us new life.

You know us all,
our wounds and our defacement.
But you know also the heavenly radiance
In which your Son's love eternally bathes us.
And so you carefully direct our footsteps.

You find no pain too great to bring us to our goal
So those whom you have chosen for companions,
To stand beside you at the eternal throne
Must stand beside you here beneath the Cross
And with hearts bleeding from bitter sorrow
Purchase heavenly radiance
for the precious souls
With whom the Son of God entrusted you.

Amen.

*(Edith Stein was a Jew who became a Catholic and a Carmelite, Sr. Teresa Benedicta and who died in the Auschwitz Concentration Camp in 1942)*

# FOR THOSE SUFFERING FROM MENTAL OR NERVOUS DISORDERS

Lord, our God, you chose **St. Dympna** as patroness of those suffering from mental and nervous disorders. Please grant, Lord through the prayers of this pure, youthful martyr, relief and consolation to all who are suffering trials, and especially those for whom we pray. *(mention those for whom you wish to pray)*

We beg you, Lord, to hear the prayers of St. Dympna on our behalf. Grant, all those for whom we pray, patience in their suffering, resignation to your divine will, fill them with hope and grant them the relief and cure they so much desire. We ask this through Christ our Lord who suffered agony in the garden. Amen.

# FOR THOSE WITH CANCER

O God, you gave **St. Peregrine** the patience
to bear intense suffering while on earth.
We ask him to intercede with our heavenly
Queen that she obtain from her divine Son the
healing we seek *(for.....)* May we one day triumph
over suffering and give glory to God as we unite
with the passion of Jesus for the saving of souls.

(Our Father, Hail Mary, Glory be to the Father)

Jesus said:
*"I have come that you may have life and have it to
the full"*

*(Jn 10: 10)*

# FOR RELIEF FROM ALCOHOLISM OR DRUG ABUSE

Lord, in your servant **Matt Talbot**, you have given us a wonderful example of triumph over addiction, of devotion to duty, and of lifelong reverence for the Blessed Sacrament. May his life of prayer and penance give us courage to take up our crosses and follow in the footsteps of our Lord and Saviour, Jesus Christ.

Father, if it is your will that your servant should be glorified by the Church, make known by heavenly favours the power he enjoys in your sight. We ask this through Christ our Lord. Amen

*(Matt Talbot overcame his alcoholism and devoted his life to prayer and penance while doing his daily work)*

# for special intentions

Eternal Father, I thank you for the grace you gave to your servant **Edel Quinn**, of striving to live always in the joy of your presence, for the radiant charity infused into her heart by your Holy Spirit, and for the strength she drew from the Bread of Life, to labour until death for the glory of your name, in loving dependence on Mary, Mother of the Church.  Confident, O merciful Father, that her life was pleasing to you, I beg you to grant me, through her intercession, the special favour I now implore....and to make known by miracles the glory she enjoys in Heaven, so that she may be glorified also by your church on earth, through Christ our Lord. Amen

We place our petition in the hands of Mary to whom Edel turned in every need. Hail Mary.....

*(Edel Quinn, lay missionary, died in Africa at the age of 37)*

# PRAYER TO THE
# HOLY FAMILY

Jesus, Mary and Joseph,
I give you my heart and my soul.

Jesus, Mary and Joseph,
Assist me now and in my last agony

Jesus, Mary and Joseph,
may I breathe forth my soul
in peace with you.

Amen

*(These prayers are often said for a happy death)*

Infant Jesus meek and mild
Look on me your little child
Pity mine and pity me
and suffer me to come to thee.

Amen

# prayer for the dead

*Jesus said: I am the resurrection and the life. If anyone believes in me, even though they die, they will live and whoever lives and believes in me will never die.*

*(Jn 11:25,26)*

Lord God
as you are the source of mercy and wish
all to be saved, have mercy on our deceased
relatives and friends (names).
Through the intercession
of Mary our Mother and all the saints bring
them to the fullness of eternal joy.
Through Christ our Lord.

Amen

*Happy are those who die in the Lord.*
*Happy indeed the Spirit says;*
*now they can rest forever after their work,*
*since their good deeds go with them.*

*(Rev 14:13)*

# thoughts on prayer

*"Pray all the time, asking for what you need, praying in the Spirit on every possible occasion'*

(Eph 6:18)

ST TERESA OF AVILA SAYS
*"Prayer is intimate conversation with the one we know loves us"*

THERE ARE MANY FORMS OF PRAYER
Blessing and Adoration
Petition and Intercession
Thanksgiving and Praise

THERE ARE MANY WAYS OF PRAYING
- Silent Prayer • Aspirations *(Short prayers)*
- Vocal Prayer • Charismatic Prayer
- Liturgical Prayer • Novenas
- Shared Prayer
- Prayer before the Blessed Sacrament
- Meditation
- Contemplation
- Centering Prayer
- Lectio Divina *(Praying with Scriptures)*

# jesus taught his disciples to pray

Jesus said to his disciples:

"In your prayers do not babble as the pagans do, for they think that by using many words they will make themselves heard. Do not be like them; your Father knows what you need before you ask him.

So you should pray like this:-

Our Father in heaven, may your name be held holy, your kingdom come, your will be done, on earth as in heaven. Give us today our daily bread. And forgive us our debts, as we have forgiven those who are in debt to us. And do not put us to the test, but save us from the evil one.

Yes, if you forgive others their failings, your heavenly Father will forgive you yours; but if you do not forgive others, your Father will not forgive your failings either."

(Mt 6: 7-15)

# A REFLECTION ON THE OUR FATHER

OUR FATHER WHO ART IN HEAVEN
God the Father is the supreme being who created all things, who always was and will be.

HALLOWED BE THY NAME
Holy and revered is the name of God. The first commandment states "I am the Lord your God. You shall not have false gods before me".

THY KINGDOM COME
When Jesus was interrogated by Pontius Pilate he asked him "Are you a King?", Jesus replied "Yes I am a King, but my kingdom is not of this world".

THY WILL BE DONE ON EARTH AS IT IS HEAVEN
We pray that God the Father's will be done here on earth as it is already done in heaven. We pray that we may know and do God's will in our daily lives.

## GIVE US THIS DAY OUR DAILY BREAD

This is a request to God the Father to provide us with the Bread of Life in the Eucharist and with our basic human needs of food, clothing, and shelter. *"But you must not set your hearts on things to eat and things to drink; nor must you worry. Your father well knows you need them. No, set your hearts on his Kingdom, and these other things will be given to you as well."*

*(Lk 12:29-31)*

## AND FORGIVE US OUR TRESPASSES

This part of the prayer is an acknowledgement of our sinful condition and a request to God the Father to forgive us. Jesus came on earth, lived, suffered and died to save us. We are forgiven in the name of Jesus when we confess our sins, receive absolution, and promise to amend our lives.

AS WE FORGIVE THOSE WHO TRESPASS AGAINST US

Just as God has forgiven our sins so we must forgive others. When Jesus was dying on the cross he said 'Father, forgive them for they know not what they do" Jesus set the example and many more have followed that way of forgiving family, friends, neighbours and even enemies who have hurt or injured them.

AND LEAD US NOT INTO TEMPTATION BUT DELIVER US FROM EVIL

We are often tempted to sin and turn from the ways of God. We are weak and easily led into temptation. Our souls still hunger for what is right and we ask God to lead us away from temptations and the ways of evil so that we can live in peace and in his grace.

AMEN

So be it ! Praise and honour and glory to our God and Father forever and ever Amen.

# lectio divina

(Prayerful reading of scripture. This can be done personally or in a group)

- Choose a text from Scripture
  ( e.g. Sunday reading)
- Opening Prayer to the Holy Spirit
- Slow attentive reading of the word of God
- Pause for silence and reflection
- Read text again
- Relate the text to other biblical texts
- Choose a word or phrase
- Read again (and share with a group)
- Pray with the text. Apply it to life
- Hold a word or phrase to memorise and contemplate

# when we cannot pray

A sudden death in the family, bad news about hospital tests, worry about children, business, or reputation and people say " I cannot pray" As we listen to their story we discover that they are really praying in a more profound way because now their prayer comes straight from the heart, Their plea is in their own words or in their very desire for divine assistance.

*"The Spirit comes to help us in our weakness. For when we cannot choose words in order to pray properly, the Spirit himself expresses our plea in a way that could never be put into words and God who knows everything in our hearts knows perfectly well what he means and that the pleas of the saints expressed by the Spirit are according to the mind of God. We know that by turning everything to their good God co-operates with all those who love him, with all those that he has called according to his purpose. For I am certain of this: neither death nor life, no angel, no prince, nothing that exists, nothing still to come, not any power, or height or depth, nor any created thing, can come between us and the love of God made visible in Christ Jesus our Lord."*

Romans 8:26-28:38

# st thérèse's thoughts on prayer

"I do as a child would do when I cannot pray. I just say what I want to say to God, quite simply, and he never fails to understand. For me prayer is an uplifting of the heart, a glance towards heaven,
a cry of gratitude and love in times of sorrow as well as joy. It is something noble, something supernatural, which expands the soul and unites it to God. When my state of spiritual aridity is such that not a single good thought will come, I repeat very slowly the Our Father and the Hail Mary, which are enough to console me and provide food for my soul."

(St. Thérèse)

# a promise of hope

I know the plans I have for you
plans for peace, not disaster,
reserving a future full of hope
for you, then when you call to
me I will listen to you.
When you seek me you will find
me, when you seek me with all your
heart:  I will let you find me.

(Jer 29:11-14)

# PRAYER OF THANKSGIVING

God our Father,
open our eyes to see your hand at work
in the splendour of creation,
in the beauty of human life.
Touched by your hand our world is holy.
Help us to cherish the gifts that surround us,
to give thanks for your love,
and share your blessings with others,
that we may experience the joy of life
in your presence.  Amen

*I want you to be happy,
always happy in the Lord
if there is anything you need,
pray for it, asking God for it
with prayer and thanksgiving*

(Phil 4:4-7)

# the Divine Praises

Blessed be God
Blessed be his Holy Name
Blessed be Jesus Christ, true God and true Man
Blessed be the name of Jesus
Blessed be his most Sacred Heart
Blessed be his most Precious Blood
Blessed be Jesus in the most Holy Sacrament of
the altar
Blessed be the Holy Spirit, the Paraclete
Blessed be the great Mother of God, Mary most
holy
Blessed be her most holy and Immaculate
Conception
Blessed be her glorious Assumption
Blessed be the name of Mary, Virgin and Mother
Blessed be St. Joseph, her most chaste spouse
Blessed be God in his Angels and in his Saints

# the brown scapular
## of our lady of mount carmel

### the scapular is a sign of mary

One of the signs in the tradition of the Church from many centuries ago is the Brown Scapular of Our Lady of Mount Carmel. It is a sign approved by the Church and accepted by the Carmelite Order as an external sign of love for Mary, of the trust her children have in her and of commitment to live like her.

### the blessed virgin teaches us

• to be open to God and to his will, shown to us in the events of our lives;

• to listen to the Word of God in the Bible and in life, to believe in it and to put into practice its demands.

• to pray at all times, as a way of discovering the presence of God in all that is happening around us.

• to be involved with people, being attentive to their needs.

## SOME PRACTICAL RULES

- People are enrolled in the Scapular only once, by a priest or authorised person.

- The Scapular can be replaced afterwards by a medal which has on one side the image of the Sacred Heart of Jesus and on the other, the image of Mary.

- The Scapular holds us to live as authentic Christians in line with the teaching of the Gospel, to receive the sacraments, to profess our special devotion to the Blessed Virgin, which should be expressed each day, at least, by saying the Hail Mary three times.

## SHORT FORM FOR GIVING THE SCAPULAR

*(by a priest)*

Receive this Scapular, a sign of your special relationship with Mary the Mother of Jesus, whom you pledge to imitate. May it be a reminder to you of your dignity as a Christian, in serving others and imitating Mary. Wear it as a sign of her protection and of belonging to the family of Carmel, voluntarily doing the will of God and devoting yourself to building a world true to his plan of community, justice and peace.

# A BLESSING

His love enfold you
His strength sustain you
His courage
Breathe upon your soul
And when the darkness comes
When earth's last tapers
flicker in the storm
His light be yours
His heart, His will, His peace
His light, His love, His Godhead
Yours,
Always

...ttle Therese of the ...

...hort life on earth became ...

...ove strong as death and of ...

God, now that you rejoice ...

...ast a glance of pity on me a...

...verything in your hands. ...

Speak a word ... me to O...

Queen of H... who smil...

...er as Queen of the Heart o...

...owerful intercession the gr...

...his moment. (Petition) ...

...lessing that may strengthe...